Sleeping Things

Sleeping Things

Poems

Holly Iglesias

Press 53
Winston-Salem

Press 53, LLC
PO Box 30314
Winston-Salem, NC 27130

First Edition

Cover design by Kevin Morgan Watson

Cover art, "Origami Crane," Copyright © 2014
by Dawn Surratt, used by permission of the artist.

Author photo by Candice Maliska

Library of Congress Control Number
2018930422

Printed on acid-free paper
ISBN 978-1-941209-76-9

¿Y si la muerte es la muerte,
qué será de los poetas
y de las cosas dormidas
que ya nadie las recuerda?

And if death is death,
what then of poets
and of sleeping things
that no one remembers
anymore?

—Federico García Lorca

The author wishes to thank the editors of the following publications where many of these poems first appeared, sometimes in a slightly different form.

75 Artful Days of Summer (North Carolina Arts Council, online): "The Mute Hysterics of Mayflower Lane"
Asheville Poetry Review: "Kicks"
The Collagist (online): "Epic of the Material World"
Fruta Bomba (chapbook, Q Avenue Press): all of the poems in section II
Hands-On Saints (chapbook, Quale Press): "Raising the Stakes"
Headwaters: "Dodge"
Luna: "Tío Builds a Bridge"
Let's Talk About Summer: International Poems, (Gino Leinweber, editor, Verlag Expeditionen): "Father, Won't You Carry Me, Carry Me" and "House of Pies, August, 1972"
New Orleans Review (online): "White Flight" and "Hit Parade"
Nothing to Declare: A Guide to the Flash Sequence (Robert Alexander, editor, Marie Alexander Poetry Series): "Prop List," "Plomo," "Nothing to Declare," "Aguacero," Triste Tropique," and "Shadow of All Things"
Palaver: "Rugbeaters" and "Plaza San Miguel"
Poem-a-Day (Academy of American Poets, online): "I Can Afford Neither"
Poetry in a Time of Chaos (Maureen Seaton and Neil de la Flor, editors): "Reliquary," "The Game of Crones," "Word Bank," and "Angelus Novus"
Poor Yorick (online): "Angelus Novus" and "The Battle Between Carnival and Lent"
Punctuate (online): "Magisterium, 1950," "Small World," "Parochial," and "Pershing Avenue, 1960"
Xavier Review: "Suffer Little Children" and "Forbid Them" "Not, Substitutions & Equivalents," and "Remote Control"

CONTENTS

III.

I.

STURDY CHILD

1.

St. Louis spring—cloth coats unbuttoned, cotton socks, oxfords, galoshes. Rows of chairs on a concrete slab, a launching pad, perhaps, or a playground. The crowd, like the photo that captures it, is black and white, a mixture of young and old, of hatted and bareheaded, each aching to settle again after years of flight.

2.

A girl in the front row waits, chin on fist, leaning forward, her inclination exposing the chair-back to mid-morning light, making it a wing, a single wing at her right shoulder. Surely by day's end her patience will be rewarded with the other one.

3.

Walking home, she reads the sign—*Children Playing*— the children illustrated bearing no resemblance to her. They are from another era, another place; they wear knickers and caps, swing books from a leather strap. She raises her face to the sky and prays for a sign that suits her own times—Telstar, Our Lady of Sorrows, Sonic Boom.

THE FRUITS OF PRAYER ARE MANY,
THE FRUITS OF THE FLESH ARE FEW

The body sojourns but briefly in the material world, a pilgrim unsure of her welcome as she dons a flimsy gown, sits at a bare table, pokes a spoon into the bowl of canned peaches.

She dreams of dusty saints, barefoot on a path, of a grotto by a stream and children on their knees. They could be ceramic, they could be flesh and bone—either way, there is danger, time to move on, to stay ahead of the advancing troops.

IN MY DAY A PENNY WENT SOMEWHERE

How I love the phrase *things were different then*, mostly
for the *things* part but also for the *then*. Before I had a
past, adults spoke of theirs, softly, in snippets: *Found
her letters in his helmet. The ring in a box in the linen closet.
Never saw him again.* Then Alaska became a state, and
we debated Automation and Godless Communism in
Civics, and, sooner than now seems possible, things
flew by, too fast to grasp—hootenannies, race riots,
Dippity-Do.

SMALL WORLD

The garage sits at the corner of the yard, a kingdom
with tiger lilies for a border.

Fathers come and go; mothers stay and stay.

Windows open, the common clatter floats out—radio,
vacuum, squalling baby.

The Friesens have a grandmother at their house, the
Spacks a bachelor.

Each night I pray one Hail Mary for good grades, one
for a vocation, and one for miniature golf.

PAROCHIAL

We were a system, a sociology, a discipline of black and white, its strictures softened by Gregorian chant and myrrh, by the nuns pacing left and right as they tapped the maps with a flourish—*Holy Roman Empire, Barbarian Invasions, Counter-Reformation.* Each parish a planet with its own orbit and priest and uniform and yet a mere speck in the cosmos, a split second in an eternity so vast that we swooned at the very notion.

WE INTERRUPT OUR REGULAR PROGRAMMING

Sunrise Semester Farm Report Three Stooges *Take Cover Immediately* Captain Kangaroo Romper Room Who Do You Trust *Dive Under a Desk* People Are Funny Deputy Dog Father Knows Best *Hide Under a Sofa* Search for Tomorrow Truth or Consequences Guiding Light *Face a Corner* As the World Turns General Hospital Edge of Night *Tuck Knees into Chest* To Tell the Truth Mister Wizard News and Weather *Block the Entrance* Ground Zero Beat the Clock Andy Griffith Show *Control Vermin* Name That Tune Quiz-a-Catholic Day in Court *Turn on Your Radio* Shock Wave The Price Is Right Dobie Gillis *Eat Perishables First* The Outer Limits Love of Life Queen for a Day *Dispose Waste Quickly* The Breaking Point Big Movie The Lord's Prayer.

HIROSHIMA FLATS

First a February tornado, prepping the area as though
it were a surgical field, then the wrecking balls and
bulldozers shoving away the rubble that once had been
sweet shop shoe shop barber shop millinery grocery
tavern church school tenement house doctor's office
dentist's office funeral parlor chili parlor bakery union
hall beauty salon drugstore five thousand structures
twenty thousand souls set again upon the migrant's
path carts piled with quilts and chairs and pots and
pans and cardboard boxes of photographs and
baptismal records the highway cutting through what
had been their neighborhood Novas Bel-Airs
Fleetwoods Falcons Galaxies Country Squires choking
the lanes the air fouled with exhaust.

EPIC OF THE MATERIAL WORLD

Candles flickering before the Infant of Prague, a nickel for small ones, a dime for large. The calendar filled with saints, with virgins and martyrs, cripples and bishops, flagellants and hysterics. The Sacred Heart bloody in a tangle of thorns, Mary's pierced with a sword. Children on their knees reciting acts of faith, of hope and charity, of conversion and reparation. Children, it is always children, small mouths, small eyes eyeing the proliferation—glass-bead rosaries, Miraculous Medals, Mass cards for the faithful departed.

GESUNDHEIT

They say we are children of a new world, a world
without war, our enemies now our friends. On the wall
a clock, a cross and the Holy Childhood calendar,
April's illustration one of a boy in a robe emitting a
faint light inside a carpenter's shop. I giggle, imagining
him sneezing from the sawdust—this Jesus tucked in
a corner with hammers and chisels, this child who
sensed the coming of a world divided, heaven from
earth, rich from poor—until Sister Rose Gemma
demands that I stand and tell the class what could
possibly be funny about a picture of our soon-to-be-
crucified Lord.

THE ROAD TO CANA

A woman in a blue serge suit wends her way through aisles of blenders and percolators, past a bank of washers and Frigidaires bulging with plastic hams and gelatin molds. The salesman leans against a Bendix like he's waiting for the bus, the machine gurgling, socks sloshing around behind the porthole. At the sight of her he straightens up, pops a mint into his mouth, and soon he is explaining the warranty—*it'll last a lifetime!*— as the machine lurches into spin cycle.

SUFFER THE LITTLE CHILDREN
AND FORBID THEM NOT

Miracles are not visited upon the desirous—the bleeding palm, the lapful of roses, the shimmering apparition. These are for the pure of heart, the poor in spirit, for peasants and shepherds, not, it seems, for people like us. But on the last day of school, a statue arrives, bought with the rolls of pennies and jars of dimes saved by the children year after year since the war ended, a golden giant, our Blessed Mother, Mary, the Queen of Peace, descending from heaven onto the roof before our very eyes.

A CHILD'S BOOK OF KNOWLEDGE:
00.1—00.3

00.1   THINGS
      00.1.1 Food
      00.1.2 Shelter
      00.1.3 Clothing
      00.1.4 Books

00.2   PEOPLE
      00.2.1 Men and Boys
            00.2.1.1 Fathers and Sons
            00.2.1.2 Uncles and Nephews
            00.2.1.3 Bosses and Workers
            00.2.1.4 Priests
            00.2.1.5 Popes
            00.2.1.6 Anti-Popes
            00.2.1.7 Heretics
      00.2.2 Women and Girls
            00.2.2.1 Mothers and Daughters
            00.2.2.2 Aunts and Nieces
            00.2.2.3 Secretaries and Nurses
            00.2.2.4 Nuns
            00.2.2.5 Virgin Martyrs
            00.2.2.6 Stigmatics

CUBAN MISSAL CRISIS

Mother bought a TV on credit to watch the Valachi hearings and *Queen for a Day*. Father fumed—it was almost World War III. In school we drew maps of the new states and awaited the thrill of air-raid drills. Priests faced us from the altar and spoke in English. We revered refugees as saints, weeping over photos of the East German boy shot in the back as he tried to flee to the West.

WHITE FLIGHT

1.

My mother lost her past in 1960; her mother never did.

2.

In the previous century, St. Louis drew its boundary, encapsulating a history that still festers between the river and Forest Park like a cyst.

3.

Driving into the city, passengers lock their doors, former GI's and their brides who fled the city in cloth coats now trolling for bebop in herringbone blazers and mink stoles.

REMORSE

Oh, victim soul, don't bite back. Instead, sink deeper and deeper into the bed, into sheets thin as pity, pillows flattened by the weight of piety. Heaven's the gate you must trudge toward with practiced patience, even as visitors ogle you, stroke your fevered brow, all the while pocketing strands of hair or crumbs from the plate you refuse, day in, day out.

MAGISTERIUM, DOUBLE NEGATIVES, AND THE EXERCISE OF POWER

While the doctrines of Cold War may be suspect, there can be no doubt that the Blessed Mother, upon completion of her earthly life, was assumed, body and soul, into heaven.

*

To *ex cathedra* teachings must be added those that are non-infallible, which also require submission. Sisters are to strive without ceasing to harness the unruly self and keep the world at bay.

*

At some point the parallels begin to manifest—Iron Curtain/iron lung, Lourdes water/processed cheese.

SUBSTITUTIONS AND EQUIVALENTS

Mother is the superior of our kitchen, her habit an apron. All around the block, block after block, women work in cells of domestic devotion, lipstick in one pocket, rosary in another, shaping their days from ground chuck and Green Stamps and re-soled shoes.

After Mass, the husbands smoke on the church steps, fingering spare change as their wives, in Sunday hats and cotton gloves, speak with Father, who sports a green chasuble for Ordinary Time and a downtown haircut.

THE CHILD'S BOOK OF KNOWLEDGE:
00.5—00.6

00.5:   MYSTERIES
        00.5.1   Irregular Verbs
        00.5.2   Veronica's Veil
        00.5.3   Negative Numbers
        00.5.4   Stigmata
        00.5.5   Dangling Participles
        00.5.6   Diminished Fifths
        00.5.7   Grace Notes
        00.5.8   Limbo
        00.5.9   Slang

00.6:   ODDITIES
        00.6.1   Notions
        00.6.2   Dry Goods
        00.6.3   Baby Teeth
        00.6.4   Scapular
        00.6.5   Pez
        00.6.6   Buffalo Nickel
        00.6.7   Itching Powder
        00.6.8   Merit Badges

PERSHING AVENUE, 1960

Mother recites "Lead, Kindly Light" to her mother,
my mother at the edge of the bed, her mother in the
middle under a white wool blanket where she has lain
for weeks, rosary in hand, the shades drawn to spare
her eyes, to soften the fact of a bed in the dining room,
her body like a cloudbank on the horizon. Her mother
drifting into sleep, my mother puts the book down,
steps out to the fire escape and smokes, ashes drifting
down to the streetcar tracks, though the streetcar itself
is long gone, the street's old name too. Again inside,
her father boiling coffee, her brother playing solitaire,
she resumes the poem—to wake her mother, adjust
the pillows, coax a sip of water. And when she falters,
when she has to turn away, her mother, fever-radiant,
sits up and finishes it for her.

YELLOW AMERICAN

Choices were limited—7-Up or Coke, one scoop or two—though we saw them as vast, whiling our time away at the drugstore, laughing too loud as we read notes scribbled on our cuffs during American Problems. A couple at the end of the counter glared at us over chipped mugs of coffee, he in madras, she in seersucker, their war behind them, ours manifesting somewhere far from the living-room TV, turned off the instant there was a snarling dog or a body bag.

RAISING THE STAKES

Upon confessing I had nothing to confess, the priest
screeched *Pride!* through the grate and pronounced me
excommunicate. The grandeur of possibilities soothed
my shame. Should I stand shoeless for days in Alpine
snow like a penitent emperor? Flick the interdict from
the sleeve of my soul, haughty as an anti-Pope at
Avignon? Briefly I prayed he thought me a boy, cocky,
in need of a crop against the cheek, not another girl,
shorn and hungry for argument, playing with the fire
that reduces flesh to its rightful station.

SISTERHOOD IS POWERFUL

Sisters drink coffee like our mothers, staring into cups to conjure the day ahead, the ghosts of Martha and Mary banging around the kitchen, each instructive, each with a part to play, everything hallowed, pie pan, pea pod, and dish rag alike.

Sisters deposit dimes and watches and tape measures deep in the dark of their pockets, for although faith fuels action, calculation, too, has its place—the perimeter of a pumpkin patch, the depth of a trench, the years to come clean in Purgatory—a vast system of debit and credit, of deed and desire, that will gain us Heaven.

REMOTE CONTROL

On saintless days, those sad ellipses on the church calendar, we pray to pure space, that place where the future blooms, our mortal souls loosed into a cool blue void, each isolate, the Mystical Body reduced to parts—ear, thumb, thigh—then flung into orbit with the monkeys and cosmonauts. Language freed from schoolbooks—*Run and see! Oh, run and see!*—pages disintegrating at the speed of light.

HIT PARADE

It began with *Gunsmoke*, with Wind Song cologne and Perry Como records, with the grandparents on tree-lined streets dying one by one, all of them, then all the little girls in white dresses going to church, and all the presidents, and all the colored men marching into history as an incessant *now* glowed on small screens in every living room, dogs off the leash, the flag in flames, murder bloating to massacre as though a single bullet wanted us all, the coed bleeding into the grass of an Ohio hillside and the naked child on fire on the other side of the world, running toward the camera, our entire past melting into abstraction.

II.

You have showed your people hard things—
you have made us to drink of the wine of astonishment.

—Psalm 60

PLOMO

No words precede the reef, none follow. Only sea fans,
brain coral, clouds above the surface. Glint of sun, of
barracuda and baitfish in flight, the Gulf Stream
sweeping by, squeezing between Florida and Cuba, the
true Cuba, the solid one, not the liquid allure of dreams.
Ahead, the drop where the sea floor sinks and the mask
begins to press its mark into your face.

SHADOW OF ALL THINGS

Dos patrias tengo yo—Cuba y la noche.
Two countries have I—Cuba and the night.
— José Martí

Cloudbank flecked peach, ochre, orchid, day dancing with night, the old world with the new. Body, ocean, melody, all of it fading to a shade neither gray nor blue. Strains of a distant bolero, the seduction more breeze than gust, a hat with a veil, say, or a lipstick called New Bruise.

TALKING IN ITALICS

After mimicry but before fluency, a straddle between the literal and the improvisational, the untrained mouth racing ahead of its governess.

Lists are safe—*jamón, leche, pan*—sentences fraught. The butcher flushes, unable to make sense of the chirping insult—*These chops are crap*—the pharmacist just raises one eyebrow—*More tablets, please, I'm spinning.*

ANTHEM

Babies—may they nap in a hammock may they be
swaddled in song may they know neither hurt nor
harm. Teach oh teach the children well and feed them
on your dreams incense applesauce zwieback bombs
because the past is just a goodbye.

FOUND:
THE STUDY GUIDE

Sec. 1. Assassination can seldom be employed with a clear conscience. Persons who are morally squeamish should not attempt it.

Sec. 4. The assassin needs the qualities of a clandestine agent—determined, courageous, intelligent, resourceful. Except in terrorist assassinations, it is desirable that the assassin be transient in the area.

Sec. 7. Bombs can provide safety and overcome guard barriers. The charge must be very large; a small or moderate explosive charge is unreliable and prone to kill the wrong man. In addition to the moral aspects, the death of casual bystanders can often produce unfavorable public reactions.

TÍO BUILDS A BRIDGE

¡Abre, niña! These teeth have forced me to open up time and again, and now it's Tío's turn to coax my jaws apart, his instruments on a TV tray next to the Naugahyde recliner in his living room. A second-wave refugee in a city where the first wave wants nothing more than to forget, Tío hums to Bola Nieve records as he works, packing my gums, preparing the incisor to anchor the bridge. I brace for pain, for a shock from the drill, for the bit to hit pulp. The room spins. I drool. He whistles for Tía to bring more cotton balls and a café con leche. At last he nods to a Flintstones glass of water and to the wastebasket where I should spit, then tilts my head up for inspection. *¡Perfecto!*

LLORONA

Abuela clanked the spoon back and forth inside a cup of café con leche at my kitchen table every Saturday and Sunday morning for twenty years. She wore a vaguely pastel cotton shift for which there remains no translation, and addressed her cup: too weak, too strong, too hot, too cool. She blamed my pots, my stove, American milk, air conditioning, the litany of complaint fouling the air, and by 8:00 a.m. the fruit had bruised, the dishcloth soured, and mites began hatching in the flour.

LA CHARADA CUBANA: A WORLD OF THINGS

The goat, a bee, six nuns by the sea,
  El capitán guapo bicycling.
The cat, the sky, *un caracol*,
  Maleta, corbata, an angry bull.
Whip, *payaso*, a basket of eels,
  Palm fronds, lightning, St. Catherine's wheel.
Matanzas, machete, shark, snake,
  Cachimba, paloma, the fiery lake.
Bruja, ladle, monkey, whore,
  Three hens, *Fortuna* behind the closed door.
Gallo, braggard, *asesino*, runt,
  Sapo, lengua, the shoes of a dunce.
Cuchillo, limón, a queen on her stool,
  Tijera, bananas, *ratones*, the Fool.
River, *araña, pluma*, remorse,
  Conejo, cochino, Death on a horse.

BICENTENARIO

We've come a long way babies and me to a place where
yellow ribbons bedeck the palm trees and day leaches
into night and summer into every season where I lift
the matted hair of my sweet sweaty babies and blow
on their necks because the heat rises before even they
do a quiet hour purple then pink until the thud of a
garbage truck the thump of a dumpster jars the babies
from sleep Doctor my eyes my ears a flash the roar my
body across them like a blanket the rain was glass was
metal the thunder a car door through the window
shrieking smoke Doctor their tiny hands.

AGUACERO

Another afternoon cloudburst and nothing to do but
wait. It will pass, as it passes in Cartagena, Cienfuegos,
Port-au-Prince, in all the humid hubs of the Caribbean.
Being half sugar, Cubans stay inside, they say, so they
don't melt.

In the battle between Amnesia and Nostalgia, Nostalgia
always wins, memories of home solid as green plantains
and gunmetal, Amnesia but a vapor passing through
the transom unannounced.

FOUND:
THE DOCTRINE OF PLAUSIBLE DENIABILITY

The concept of Miami was correct, but got out of hand. An armada of private planes and boats, lots of C-4—we had a disposal problem. ● You need hard proof. Bombs consume the evidence and victims don't cooperate (I mean the ones who survive). No one will name names. ● It's hard to get the attention of the American people. The slaying is a good lesson, it shows the tail of the immediate future. The beast is but a little way ahead. ● *They bought the chain, but not the monkey*, says Bosch, who some call freedom fighter instead of terrorist. ●

TRISTE TROPIQUE

1.

You depend so on the machete to keep the strangler
figs at bay.

2.

Forgive me—the plums gone, my letters in the icebox
now—I can't sleep, the machete under your pillow
so cold.

THE LOVE THERE THAT'S SLEEPING

A Charlie Brown Christmas soothed us like it once soothed my parents, who beckoned their children to the couch to ingest the cartoon as an antidote to acid rock. Thirty years later, they were gone, their stories of the good fight and the joys of a two-bedroom ranch buried with them on a bluff above the river. The story to bury with me will be that of scribbling a chord progression from *The White Album* over and over on the back of a grocery list, the pattern a sedative to dull the news of the death of a boy I loved by his own hand during the *Bob Hope Bicentennial Special.*

SUCIO

The boy, crying, clutches the neck of his rescuer as a federal agent in riot gear yanks him away. Each custody case is a dirty war, this one no different, the child held for ransom. The mother floats somewhere offshore, a body tangled in seaweed near a tax-sheltered island, perhaps. The father arrives to claim his boy plucked miraculously from the sea, abuelas across the hemisphere weeping at private altars of betrayal.

THEN, AS DID WE

The Wall finally fell, chipped away piece by piece, the
war cold as ever on the streets of Miami.

PROP LIST

Near the end, there were cinch belts, stilettos, guayaberas, two-carat studs, crystal ashtrays. I still had children and was free of disease. An undocumented woman ironed in the garage all day, the same shirts over and over, and a man came every other week to shock the pool with lithium hypochlorite. They may tell you I left of my own accord, but observe what happens should someone pass me wearing Drakkar Noir.

MORIR SOÑANDO

Near the Malecón, the image of a gaunt Fidel fills an outdoor screen, the crowd offering prayers for him for the cameras while reciting in silence the names of those who fled, a baroque litany of exodus and the impending tide of return.

In Miami, the mass excavation begins, a scramble through half a century of shirts from the refugee center, bus-boy aprons, designer jeans, deeds in English, deeds in Spanish, urns of ashes.

Ninety miles between them, a strait of common grief, *la isla imaginaria* washing away with the debris of revolution.

III.

Live among your dead,
whom you have every right to love.

—Brenda Marie Osbey

FATHER, WON'T YOU CARRY ME, CARRY ME

The first time I saw the Mississippi from the air, I knew my place, and I knew that home was a sinuous ribbon lacing east to west, past to future, bondage to possibility, appearing and disappearing like a snake in new-mown hay as the sun flashed on its surface. Many times I have crossed the bridge that takes me home then takes me away, by car, by train, and even on foot, the current electric beneath me as St. Louis crouches on the western bank like a weary roustabout. Each spring the river swells there, rolls out of its ancient bed to sweep away all that is dead or forgotten, all that is foolish or weak, the debris tumbling inevitably south—spinet and spire, cottonwood and calf.

RUGBEATERS

A winter's worth of dust and crumbs and all that fell to
the floor in the hush of great-grandfather's version of
grace, heads bowed over soup that lost its warmth while
he implored the Lord to make of each earthly thing an
object lesson, admonishing his children to regard even
the broth as instructive, which of course it was, the dill-
scented steam teaching them all they needed to know
of patience and the powers of appetite. By afternoon,
the boy at his desk, sipping cocoa from a Dresden cup,
reading the leather-bound books that signaled
entitlement while his sisters beat the last of ten carpets
on the lawn, giddy with exhaustion.

DOODLES AND DODE

They come toward me, then stop, stooping down, opening their arms like two pairs of parentheses, gumdrops in his left hand, a hanky the color of early May in her right. The No. 56 bus has brought them here from the city, their arrival marking the Saturday I call childhood. From their coats rise the scents of their three-room flat: nutmeg, pencil shavings, Old Spice cologne.

KICKS

He needs to speculate, to provoke and spar like most
people need to breathe. Barely dawn and my old man
is ready to roll—How high's the river today, 28 feet,
30?—the question a mere launch into quickening
currents of desire. What did Mitch pay for that station
wagon? Does your mother smoke in the basement?
Were there more Jesuits in colonial Canada or Mexico?
What wiped out the settlement at Cahokia? If a
gorgeous dame sits next to you in a bar in Rome, do
you buy her a drink? How many comics do you kids
read in a week? How old will you be when I die, 30,
50? Come on, make a guess—just for the sake of kicks.

BOOKENDS

1.

Already dressed, he watches the percolator, the contraption rattling, the racket cheerful, companionable in the dark. He shakes off the last of sleep like a drenched dog with a low honeyed growl, his dreams dissolving with the sunrise.

2.

Still dressed, she sips tea, flips through pages of drapes and cakes and pill-box hats. She starts the puzzle, taps a pencil on the table like she's ready for dictation. Percolator set for tomorrow, the house finally quiet— she could sit here all night.

WORD BANK

1. *Migration* arrives in the 17th century, in reference first to people, then animals.

2. The *vagrant* lacks a fixed abode and thus wanders.

3. Coined under Louis XIV, *refugee* describes one seeking asylum—

4. We call the mid-19th century wave of revolutions *Springtime of the Peoples.*

5. But what of the Hunger and *blight* expanding from a plant disease to that which withers hope?

—then shifts during the Great War to one fleeing *home.*

THE BLUE SISTERS OF WHIMSY

One propelled by modesty, the other by desire, they progress as pilgrims from one thrift store to the next, their path by now a habit, moving from sweaters to dishes, knickknacks to books, seeking out items with depleted genealogies—metal zipper, Melmac gravy boat, Brownie handbook, mended saucer, St. Jude devotionals tied in string—their mother superior in all things but this, the fond look back.

GELATIN MOLD

Newly wed, she twirled around the kitchen in Bermuda shorts and white flats, a cigarette smoking on the windowsill above the toaster as she made scalloped potatoes and pork chops and Jell-O with Dream Whip topping.

In the years of aerosol cheese and cocktail wieners, she lost me. I turned to the raw and fibrous, hungry for hardy grains and root vegetables and a language she didn't speak. It's true: I fled, leaving her to the rib roasts and aspics quivering in silence on the kitchen table.

I CAN AFFORD NEITHER THE RAIN

Nor the strip of light between the slats, the window
itself blind with grief. Nor the bench where a mourner
lingers, the others on to the next thing, leaning into
the bar, toasting the sweethearts, gone and gone, their
desires softening now in the earth. Nor the bluff above
the Mississippi where centuries of veterans rest, where
stands the stone that bears their names, the wind of
romance hard against it.

RELIQUARY

It was still life after she'd gone—hair in the brush,
scented talc, the impress of her younger self in the
cushions of the couch. Her departure called for elegy,
which swelled with great speed into epic, until it burst
and, exhausted, fell, settling like a tissue-wrapped ringlet
slipped free from the pages of *Sonnets from the Portuguese*.

THE BATTLE BETWEEN CARNIVAL AND LENT

From a spare palette—blue, red, brown—hubbub.
Revelers and Scolds circle the Drunk straddling a barrel.
Hooligans taunt cloaked Penitents shuffling into
church. Hens squawk, maids squeal, a boy tickles the
backside of Satan. The Cripple peers into a well.
Children scatter like marbles, jostling bakers, soldiers,
dunces, and nuns all around the square. Splashes of
white form a triangle—apron, grain sack, goose egg—
invoking the Trinity and other miracles of composition.
A single day, the ground neutral, and windows
everywhere, gaping like mouths.

LOBAL WARFARE

Destiny was manifest long before a papal bull deemed
the hemispheres discrete, the earthly lobes isolate in
function and title, dominion over the savage hordes
part and parcel of the plan of redemption. Thus in
unison did Cross and Compass rule, their exquisite
instruments yielding not one map but two, purses
bulging like the bodice of a plump strumpet.

ANGELUS NOVUS

The Angel of History must look just so.
　　　　—Walter Benjamin

To ease the pain, he evokes the Klee caged in his mind,
converting the image to text, scratching left to right,
left to right. The room reeks of romance, but this lust
for the past, for the erotics of time and its beautiful
damage, is what wounds him. He stares at her face
and she stares back, a rose window bereft of glass,
wings singed by future winds, the heap of spires and
thrones, satchels and bones, mounting at her feet.

DODGE

We bounce the baby, pass her around our circle made
of blue jeans and peasant blouses and accents that
betray us at the market. Weaning, she craves distraction,
her voice bigger than her body, a pale thing frail as our
safety here. Tomorrow at the embassy in Madrid she
will be naturalized, made a citizen of the place we fled,
her photo pasted into my compromised passport. But
tonight, I jostle her and pass her around, her cheeks
kissed again and again, the first one born to us so far
from any notion of home.

UNCIVIL WAR, ZARAGOZA, 1974

I too lost countries and homes and a river, loss no harder to master than the rigor of words, the intricacy of patterns like those knit into the shawls of abuelas who strolled down Gran Via each Sunday, grandchildren ten steps ahead, sons ten behind, husbands long gone, buried in banks of rubble along the Ebro.

FAÇADES

I expected window boxes of geraniums, a meadow maybe, half a dozen kids, a pile of white towels. I would bake pies and bathe babies, and at night read Yeats. If there were a husband, he would be in a distant land felling trees. Instead, there was a string of apartments—Crystal Courts, The Starlite, Sabal Palm—each with a pool, a laundromat, and a foyer with a bucket of plastic ivy by the welcome mat. Once a month his father took us out for Cuban-Chinese food and never left a tip. Forty years later his widow tells me that he had a girlfriend at The Starlite in those days, sighing *Ai, que hijo de puta.*

THE CHILDREN I KEEP

Trying to put to sleep as steam pipes rattle and teacups clink and now the blue moon rasping against a frosted pane. A posture of caution, ear cocked for the back door to slam, on the floor shards of objects bashed with the bat—typewriter, lamp, ceramic clown. No time to sweep up the mess, what with the snow thigh-deep and four loads of dirty laundry.

IT IS DIFFICULT TO GET THE NEWS

A yellow wall phone mounted by the back door so I could sit on the stoop to talk. Muslin curtains, dirty pot soaking in the sink, dog digging under the chicken-wire fence when it rang. The kids were across the street at school and I was sewing Halloween costumes, still trying to get it all right, spending too much time on home-made bread and lentil soup to go with the fish sticks. I wore an apron over my bell-bottoms. I taught piano lessons in the living room. I wrote my parents every week. Sheets were on the line—I watched them dry, watched them surrender the scent of soap to the autumn air, not sure why you had called or what your faltering voice might mean or why you asked if I was alone. You said the words; they registered as a thud on the other side of a foot-thick wall. You hung up; I hesitated, the receiver dangling from my shoulder, the dial tone droning.

THE GAME OF CRONES

Dungeons & Dragons pulled our children through the haze of the Reagan years. It gave them something to do as we watched TV in a jug-wine stupor—evangelists warning of end days, another tiny dictator in the Dade County jail, the dawn of aerobics. They developed plots deep into the night; their homework suffered. All we could do was peek through the blinds as helicopter searchlights strafed the neighborhood.

Tonight at the Crow & Quill Public House, post-apocalyptic youth concoct attars of the past—Weimar waifs, Dharma bums, Kewpie dolls, the last Doobie Brother—expressing in costume virtue spoiled and vice redeemed. All they need now is the lusty monk.

THE MUTE HYSTERICS OF MAYFLOWER LANE

Like peonies they droop, keeling over, letting go, each
petal gasping as it drifts down to the heap of browning
pink. By dusk the stems right themselves, naked in the
hush that drains away all color. Modesty demands it,
this leeching that teaches the soul to fade.

GRISAILLE

She scrubs the carrels, her brush knocking around the
bucket, the splash of her rag in the filthy water breaking
my concentration, the narrative blanket warming my
knees snatched away. Outside, bushes stripped of
berries, peeling bark, Mt. Pisgah a blur in the west.
The wind too is gray, March bracing for its own demise,
spring the death, the birth again and again.

PLAZA SAN MIGUEL

Across the way my past sips coffee, her cup, like mine, steaming. She is dressed as the girl in Dylan's song who never stumbles, who's got no place to fall, and I'm playing the lady in a camel-hair coat and a red pashmina that would have made my mother proud. We sit, silent, as the Spanish of Spaniards fills the square, as she jots in a notebook a beggar's plea, the whisper of lovers. I wish she would look up and see me, but there is no comforting her now, far from home, convinced that exile is an act of will, something to hone the dull contours of youth.

NOTHING TO DECLARE

The spoon of a woman dead long before your birth, daughter, sterling, the bowl demure, my great aunt's initials inscribed with a flourish at the bottom. The patina soft as that of the cream-and-sugar set my mother bought during the war, which you have. Or I suppose you do. I gave it to you when you married, when it looked as though we had made it, as though the lies and knives were things of the past. Before the new regime and the hiding of gifts.

GLOSSARY

Plomo: lead weight, sinker

Jamón, leche, pan: ham, milk, bread.

Llorona: "The Weeping Woman," a legend popular in Mexico and Central America. Also, cry-baby.

Abuela: grandmother

Charada Cubana: Cuban lottery. Also, enigma.

Capitán guapo: handsome captain

Caracol: seashell

Maleta: suitcase

Corbata: necktie

Payaso: clown

Matanzas: slaughter. Also, a province in western Cuba.

Machete: machete

Cachimba: smoking pipe. Also, empty cartridge. Also, slut.

Paloma: dove

Bruja: witch

Fortuna: Fortune

Gallo: rooster

Asesino: assassin

Sapo: toad

Lengua: tongue

Cuchillo: knife

Limón: lemon

Tijera: scissors

Ratones: mice

Araña: spider

Pluma: feather. Also, pen.

Conejo: rabbit

Cochino: pig. Also, filthy, bloody.

Bicentenario: bicentennial

Aguacero: downpour

Sucio: dirty
Morir soñando: to die dreaming
Malecón: The esplanade and sea wall that stretches from
    the mouth of Havana Harbor to Vedado
Exilio: exile
Isla imaginaria: imaginary island

"Sturdy Child"

We shall by a process of sublime irony have reached a stage in this story where safety will be the sturdy child of terror, and survival the twin brother of annihilation. (From Winston Churchill's farewell address to the House of Commons in 1955 as he pondered the era of nuclear brinksmanship.)

The photo, from the *St. Louis Post Dispatch* in 1954, shows a crowd awaiting a presentation about Pruitt-Igoe, a new federally subsidized complex of high-rise apartments that became the face of urban renewal in St. Louis. It was razed twenty years later, a nightmare in the history of public housing.

"Remorse"

A victim soul is someone chosen by God to undergo intense suffering for the salvation of others.

"Found: The Study Guide"

Excerpted from training materials for Operation PBSUCCESS, the CIA's covert mission to precipitate the 1954 coup d'etat in Guatemala. [http://nsarchive2.gwu.edu/NSAEBB/NSAEBB4/]

"Found: The Doctrine of Plausible Deniability"

Excerpted from news articles in *The Miami Herald*, *Miami New Times*, *The Nation* and *The Wall Street Journal* published in the 1970s and 1980s; from Metro-Dade Police Department reports on terrorism; and from declassified CIA documents regarding covert operations in Dade County.

Cuban exile Orlando Bosch was a pediatrician turned terrorist and CIA operative. He was given safe haven in the U.S. in 1990 by President George H.W. Bush, who as head of the CIA in 1976 had declined Costa Rica's offer to extradite Bosch.

"Bicentenario"

A car bomb was detonated near the author's apartment complex in Miami on Thanksgiving morning, November 27, 1975, and again on April 3, 1976. For a list of all bombings, compiled in 1983 by the Organized Crime Bureau of the Metro-Dade Police Department, see: cuban-exile.com/doc_001-025/doc0022.html

Heart-felt thanks to Nickole Brown for bringing my manuscript to Press 53 and introducing me to publisher and editor Kevin Watson; to my dear friends Landon Godfrey and Katherine Min, who have nurtured my mind and soul; to Maureen Seaton for her kind light and bountiful spirit; to Cyrus Cassells for an early nod that made all the difference; and especially to Robert Alexander, editor extraordinaire and generous champion.

The work in this collection was written with support from the National Endowment for the Arts, the North Carolina Arts Council, and the Master of Liberal Arts & Sciences Program at the University of North Carolina-Asheville. Research for the first section was conducted at the archives of the Archdiocese of St. Louis under the expert guidance of archivist Rena Schergen.

Holly Iglesias

Holly Iglesias is the author of two poetry collections, *Souvenirs of a Sunken World* and *Angles of Approach*, and a critical work, *Boxing Inside the Box: Women's Prose Poetry*. She has taught at University of North Carolina-Asheville and University of Miami, focusing on documentary and archival poetry, and she translated the work of Cuban poet Caridad Atencio. She is the recipient of fellowships from the National Endowment for the Arts, the North Carolina Cultural Council, the Edward Albee Foundation, and the Massachusetts Cultural Council. Her poems have appeared in many journals and in anthologies such as *The House of Your Dreams: an International Collection of Prose Poetry, Nothing to Declare: a Guide to the Flash Sequence, The Best of the Prose Poem*, and *Sweeping Beauty: Contemporary American Women Poets Do Housework*.

Cover artist Dawn Surratt studied art at the University of North Carolina at Greensboro as a recipient of the Spencer Love Scholarship in Fine Art. She has exhibited her work throughout the Southeast and currently works as a freelance designer and artist. Her work has been published internationally in magazines, on book covers, and in print media. She lives on the beautiful Kerr Lake in northern North Carolina with her husband, one demanding cat, and a crazy Pembroke Welsh Corgi.

CPSIA information can be obtained
at www.ICGtesting.com
Printed in the USA
BVOW11s1946230218
508942BV00001B/38/P